WILLIAM LLOYD

THE
SAVIOUR

A MEDITATION UPON
THE DEATH OF CHRIST
FOR TENOR & BASS SOLI
CHOIR & ORGAN

O THE REV. DERRICK GREEVES &
LL THE CHOIR OF WESTMINSTER CENTRAL HALL
ORDS SELECTED & WRITTEN BY BRYN REES

Lloyd Webber

PART ONE:
MAN'S NEED

PART TWO:
GOD'S REMEDY

1. THE LAST SUPPER

2. THE GARDEN OF GETHSEMANE

3. THE CRUCIFIXION

PART THREE:
NEW LIFE IN CHRIST

NOTE:
IT IS SUGGESTED THAT SOME
DEGREE OF RHYTHMICAL FREEDOM
SHOULD BE EXERCISED IN THE
NARRATIVE SECTIONS OF THE WORK.
L.W.

Permission to perform this work must be obtained from
The Performing Rights Society Limited, 0207 306 4455,
29/33 Berners Street, London W1P 4AA.
Telephone: 0207 580 5544, Fax: 0207 631 4138.

Original edition published (1961) by Novello & Co Limited.
This edition © copyright 1994 The Really Useful Group.
info@pro.co.uk

THE SAVIOUR

BRYN REES

PART I
MAN'S NEED

W. S. LLOYD WEBBER

BASS SOLO

There is none right-eous, no not one, none right-eous, no not one; for all have_ sin-ned and come short, come short of the glo-ry of God.

poco calmato

CHORUS

While we were yet sin-ners, Christ died for us.

While we were yet sin - ners, Christ died for us.

poco calmato

While we were yet sin - ners, Christ died for us.

(FULL)

While we were yet sin - ners, Christ died for us.

poco calmato

Man.

più agitato
BASS SOLO

The good that I would, I do not; ___ but the e - vil that I

would not, that I do. O wretch - ed man that I am, O wretch - ed

man that I am! Who ___ shall de - liv - er me? ___

Who ___ shall de - liv - er me? ___

8

CHORUS

CHORUS

Where-by can faith af - firm, af-firm That God is Love?

(FULL) *mp*

Be-

Be -

cause He gave His Son, All gifts a - bove.

Here-by God's Love is

cause He gave His Son, All gifts a - bove.

That Je - sus died for all, Up-on the

shown, For all to see; That Je - sus died, That

That Je-sus died for all, That

That Je-sus died, That

CONGREGATIONAL HYMN

ST. FRANCIS XAVIER   J. STAINER, 1840–1901

My God, I love Thee, not because
   I hope for Heaven thereby,
Nor yet because who love Thee not
   Are lost eternally.

Thou, O my Jesus, Thou didst me
   Upon the Cross embrace;
For me didst bear the nails and spear,
   And manifold disgrace.

And griefs and torments numberless,
   And sweat of agony;
Yea, death itself; and all for me
   Who was Thine enemy.

Then why, O Blessèd Jesu Christ,
   Should I not love Thee well?
Not for the hope of winning Heaven,
   Nor of escaping hell;

Not with the hope of gaining aught,
   Not seeking a reward;
But as Thyself hast lovèd me,
   O ever-loving Lord.

So would I love Thee, dearest Lord,
   And in Thy praise will sing;
Solely because Thou art my God,
   And my eternal King.

Francis Xavier, c. 1506–52
(tr. by Edward Caswell, 1814–78)

PART II
GOD'S REMEDY

1 The Last Supper

poco rall.

(TENOR) p

meno mosso

BASS mp

And He said ___ un-to them, 'This is my blood of the new

Ped.

cov-en-ant, which is shed ___ for _ ma-ny.'

CHORUS
affettuoso pp

The ta - ble ___ of the Lord is spread, His gra-cious

pp

The ta - ble of ___ the Lord is spread, His gra-cious

affettuoso
(FULL) pp

The ta - ble of the Lord is spread, His gra-cious

(FULL) pp

The ta - ble ___ of the Lord is spread, His gra-cious

affettuoso ♩=112

pp

Voices alone adlib.

Man.

2 The Garden of Gethsemane

quiet-ed with-in me, so_ dis-qui-et-ed with-in me?

Man.

più mosso

I had gone with the mul-ti-tude,_

Ped.

poco allarg.

_ I went with them to the house of God, With the voice of joy and

praise, With a mul-ti-tude that kept_ ho-ly day, With a

CHORUS

34

3 The Crucifixion

Cross, O Bless - ed, Bless - ed, O Bless - ed

ra - ther be The Man Who there Was put to shame,

rubato
pp
The Man Who there Was put to shame

meno mosso al fine
for me.'

Man. Ped. (32')

CONGREGATIONAL HYMN

ROCKINGHAM

Adapted by
E. MILLER, 1731-1807

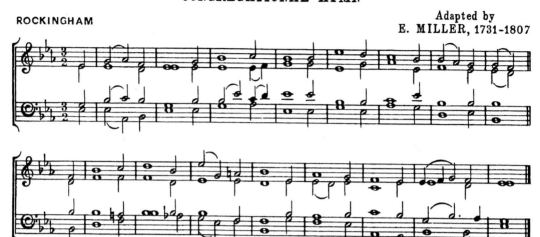

When I survey the wondrous Cross
 On which the Prince of Glory died,
My richest gain I count but loss,
 And pour contempt on all my pride.

Forbid it, Lord, that I should boast
 Save in the Cross of Christ my God;
All the vain things that charm me most,
 I sacrifice them to His Blood.

See, from His head, His hands, His feet,
 Sorrow and love flow mingled down;
Did e'er such love and sorrow meet?
 Or thorns compose so rich a crown?

Were the whole realm of nature mine,
 That were an offering far too small;
Love so amazing, so divine,
 Demands my soul, my life, my all.

Isaac Watts, 1674-1748

Optional organ part, if last verse is sung in unison.

PART III
NEW LIFE IN CHRIST

*Full, Semichorus or Solo

poco rall.   a tempo

life_ in Christ be - gins, And all_ thy sins, thy sins_ a - toned!

Man.

ALTO* p

The sav - ing act is

SOPRANO mp

Re -

(ALTO) cresc.

done, The path_ of _ mer - cy trod; Re - deemed through

Ped.

cresc.

deemed through Christ the Son, And God re - main-eth, re - main - eth

Christ the Son, And God_ re - main-eth, re - main - eth

*Full, Semichorus or Solo

(Ped.)

a tempo, ma poco meno mosso

Man.

CONGREGATIONAL HYMN

MISERICORDIA

H. SMART, 1813-79

Just as I am, without one plea
But that Thy blood was shed for me,
And that Thou bidd'st me come to Thee,
    O Lamb of God, I come.

Just as I am, though tossed about
With many a conflict, many a doubt,
Fightings and fears within, without,
    O Lamb of God, I come.

Just as I am, poor, wretched, blind,—
Sight, riches, healing of the mind,
Yea, all I need, in Thee to find,
    O Lamb of God, I come.

Just as I am, Thou wilt receive,
Wilt welcome, pardon, cleanse, relieve;
Because Thy promise I believe,
    O Lamb of God, I come.

Just as I am—Thy love unknown
Has broken every barrier down—
Now to be Thine, yea, Thine alone,
    O Lamb of God, I come.

Just as I am, of that free love
The breadth, length, depth, and height to prove,
Here for a season, then above,
    O Lamb of God, I come.

Charlotte Elliott, 1789-1871